Our World

THE MIRROR

A folk tale from Korea

Retold by Nick Harris

NATIONAL GEOGRAPHIC LEARNING

Tae Hyun, a farmer, is shopping for a present for his wife, Sun Hee.

'I would like to buy something very special,' he tells a shopkeeper.

'Buy her this mirror,' says the shopkeeper. 'You can see yourself in it.'

At this time in Korea, people did not have mirrors.

'Is that me?' asks Tae Hyun. 'I thought I was taller.'

Then he says, 'No one in my village has got one of these. This is going to be a fantastic present!'

At home, Tae Hyun puts the mirror on the wall.

'Sun Hee is going to love this present!' he says. 'The mirror will show her that she is prettier than all of the other wives in the village.'

Tae Hyun goes out to find his wife.

But Sun Hee and Tae Hyun's mother come home before Tae Hyun can find them.

Sun Hee looks in the mirror. She sees herself for the first time. She thinks it is someone else!

'My husband has got a new wife!' she says. 'She is younger than me!'

Tae Hyun's mother looks in the mirror. She sees herself for the first time, too.

'That's not a new wife!' says Tae Hyun's mother. 'It is an old woman, like me! But she is older than me! Your husband has got a new mother!'

Tae Hyun's father hears Sun Hee and his wife crying. He comes in to see what is wrong.

'Tae Hyun has got a new younger wife!' says Sun Hee.

'No. He has got a new older mother!' says Tae Hyun's mother.

Tae Hyun's father looks in the mirror. He doesn't recognise himself either.

'That isn't an old woman or a young wife,' he says. 'It's an old man, like me. But he looks stronger than me!'

'Why does Tae Hyun want a new father?' he says. 'Aren't I strong enough to help him on the farm?'

'I didn't see an old man!' says Sun Hee. 'I saw a younger and prettier woman.'

'I saw an older woman!' said Tae Hyun's mother.

Tae Hyun and Sun Hee's son comes in. 'What's wrong?' he asks.

'Look!' everyone says.

The boy looks in the mirror.

'Who's that boy?' says the son. 'He's wearing my hat! Give me my hat back!'

Finally, Tae Hyun hears his family. He runs into the house. They tell him about the new people they saw in the mirror.

'Those aren't new people!' he says. 'You saw yourselves! Look!'

'Ahh!' they all say with a smile. 'What a nice family! We are very good-looking!'

Facts About Physical Changes: Metamorphosis

The young of some animals do not look at all like the adults they become. They change completely when they become adults. This change is called **metamorphosis.**

Insect Metamorphosis

Some insects change by metamorphosis.

1 A baby butterfly hatches from an egg. A very tiny caterpillar comes out of the egg.

2 After a while, the caterpillar wraps itself in a covering called a **chrysalis.**

3 After two weeks, a butterfly comes out of the chrysalis.

Amphibian Metamorphosis

Many amphibians also change by metamorphosis.

1 A baby frog also hatches from an egg. The baby frog is called a **tadpole.** It looks like a tiny fish.

2 As time passes, the tadpole grows a head and legs. It starts to look more like a frog.

3 Finally, the frog loses its tadpole tail, and the change is complete. It is no longer a tadpole. It is a frog!

Fun with Families

Write a sentence about the circled person or animal. Use one of the words below.

taller **cuter** **older**
stronger **younger**

1. This giraffe is taller.

2. ______________________

3. ______________________

4. ______________________

5. ______________________

Write a paragraph about the family in the photo. Use a different word from the box in each sentence.

taller	older	stronger	younger

The brother is older than the sisters.

Write a few sentences about your own family using the words in the box above.

Glossary

amphibian

hatch

amphibians animals that live part of their lives in water and part of their lives on land

hatch come out of an egg

husband a married man

insect a type of small animal with a body that has three parts and three pairs of legs

recognise to see someone or something and know who that person or what that thing is

shopkeeper a person who is in charge of a shop

wife a married woman